JOY

**The Top 100 Reasons
Why Christian's Should Always
Have a Song In Their Heart
And a Spring in Their Step**

JEANIE PRICE

Star Song Publishing Group
a division of Jubilee Communications, Inc.
P.O. Box 150009
Nashville, Tennessee 37215

ISBN # 1-56233-088-8

Printed in the United States of America
First Printing, September 1993

1 2 3 4 5 6 7 8 9 – 97 96 95 94 93

INTRODUCTION

Recently my sister, Sherri, paid me a visit. We spent the morning talking about the kinds of things that sisters typically discuss: our families, our jobs, our plans for the weekend. Just a normal, everyday, run-of-the-mill conversation.

As she was about to leave I asked her how her friend, Julie, was doing. Three months earlier Julie had been diagnosed with an advanced stage of ovarian cancer. Her prognosis was grim. Most women live less than a year after this form of cancer has been detected in their bodies. Sherri sat back down and began to tell me one of the most beautiful stories of faith and courage I have ever heard.

When Sherri last visited her in the hospital Julie had just undergone another in a series of highly potent chemotherapy treatments. Despite the intense pain and severe nausea she was feeling, the only thing she could talk about was how wonderful the Lord had been to her, her husband, Greg, and their two young daughters, ages one and four. Not once did she complain about what was happening to her. She didn't voice one negative thought or express any anxiety and fear. Instead, her face glowed with an inner joy as she shared how God was answering every prayer she had for her family and how the presence of the Holy Spirit was so real that she felt nothing but peace over her situation.

Sherri later shared with me that Julie had written a letter to her high school graduating class telling them about her illness and describing her relationship with Jesus Christ—how He had been faithful, even in the darkest hours, and was demonstrating His love for her more and more each day. Her testimony had a dramatic effect. Many of her former classmates responded with letters saying that her story had caused them to reflect on their lives and that they had asked the Lord to enter their hearts.

Even though I have never met Julie, she has ministered to me as well. I think about her every time I become impatient in rush hour traffic, or worry about meeting a deadline. I think about how she has turned her cares and concerns for herself and her family into praises to God, and how He has given her what He has promised to give all His children, the peace that passes all understanding and joy unspeakable.

At some point in life everyone experiences a crisis over which they have little or no control: physical illness, depression, a broken marriage, the death of a child, the loss of a job. The Bible has a simple remedy for conquering sorrow and achieving victory over despair:

> *Always be full of joy in the Lord; I say it again, rejoice! Let everyone*
> *see that you are unselfish and considerate in all you do. Remember that*
> *the Lord is coming soon. Don't worry about anything; instead, pray*
> *about everything; tell God your needs and don't forget to thank him for*
> *his answers. If you do this you will experience God's peace, which*
> *is far more wonderful than the human mind can understand. His peace*
> *will keep your thoughts and your hearts quiet and at rest as you trust*
> *in Christ Jesus.*
>
> PHILIPPIANS 4:4-7

This book is dedicated to Julie, and others like her, who daily remind us of the joy that only God can provide. As you read each thought and verse, remember that our Lord, Jesus Christ, bore the sins and pain of a fallen world upon the cross at Calvary so that we might have the promise of eternal joy in His presence.

Your friend in Christ Jesus,

Jeanie Price
Nashville, Tennessee

Everything you do can bring you joy!

DEUTERONOMY 12:18

Rejoice before the Lord your God
in everything you do.

The Lord can solve all of your problems!

1 SAMUEL 2:1

How I rejoice in the Lord!
How he has blessed me! Now I have
an answer for my enemies,
for the Lord has solved my problem.
How I rejoice!

God's Word will be made clear to you!

NEHEMIAH 8:12

So the people went away to eat a festive meal
and to send presents;
it was a time of great and joyful celebration
because they could hear
and understand God's words.

You will be known as someone who brings joy
and laughter to others!

JOB 8:21

He will yet fill your mouth with laughter and
your lips with shouts of joy.

The misery and despair
caused by wicked people will soon come to
an abrupt end!

JOB 20:5

The triumph of the wicked
has been short-lived, and the joy of the godless
but for a moment.

God listens to your needs with infinite patience
and mercy!

JOB 23:6

Would he merely overpower me with his
greatness? No, he would listen with sympathy.

Fear and trembling take on a new and holy
meaning in the lives of Christians!

PSALMS 2:11

Serve the Lord with reverent fear;
rejoice with trembling.

The joy of the Lord is more satisfying than
a great feast!

PSALMS 4:7

Yes, the gladness you have given me is far
greater than their joys at harvest time as they
gaze at their bountiful crops.

God is defending you and your family,
right now!

PSALMS 5:11

But make everyone rejoice who puts
his trust in you. Keep them shouting for joy
because you are defending them.
Fill all who love you with happiness.

The God you serve is the one true God!

PSALMS 9:2

I will be glad, yes, filled with joy
because of you. I will sing your praises, O Lord
God above all gods.

You are one of God's children—
He will always be merciful to you!

PSALMS 13:5

But I will always trust in you and in your mercy
and shall rejoice in your salvation.

The Lord is protecting the many blessings
He has given you!

PSALMS 16:5

The Lord himself is my inheritance, my prize.
He is my food and drink,
my highest joy! He guards all that is mine.

The beauty and majesty of nature were
created just for you!

PSALMS 16:6

He sees that I am given
pleasant brooks and meadows as my share!
What a wonderful inheritance!

God cares about your physical needs and is always there to take care of you!

PSALMS 16:8-9

I am always thinking of the Lord;
and because he is so near, I never need to
stumble or to fall. Heart,
body, and soul are filled with joy.

The presence of the Lord will fill you with
exquisite pleasure!

PSALMS 16:11

You have let me experience
the joys of life and the exquisite pleasures of
your own eternal presence.

The Lord will give you
the priceless gifts of peace, satisfaction, and
contentment free of charge!

PSALMS 17:15

But as for me, my contentment is not
in wealth but in seeing you and knowing all is
well between us. And when I awake
in heaven, I will be fully satisfied, for I will see
you face to face.

As a Christian you have been freed from
the confusion and chaos of this world; move
ahead in life with confidence!

PSALMS 19:7-8

God's laws are perfect. They protect us, make us
wise, and give us joy and light.

Even the rulers of this earth are in awe over
the strength of our Lord!

PSALMS 21:1

How the king rejoices in your strength, O Lord!
How he exults in your salvation.

God freely gives us the righteous desires
of our hearts!

PSALMS 21:2

For you have given him his heart's desire,
everything he asks you for!

You do not have to search for happiness;
God has promised it to you for eternity!

PSALMS 21:6

You have endowed him with
eternal happiness. You have given him the
unquenchable joy of your presence.

The Holy Spirit will keep you from
stumbling into sin!

PSALMS 26:12

I publicly praise the Lord for keeping me from
slipping and falling.

You are not alone,
God is standing between you and every danger!

PSALMS 28:7

He is my strength, my shield
from every danger. I trusted in him, and he
helped me. Joy rises in my heart
until I burst out in songs of praise to him.

God will dry your tears and turn your
weeping into laughter!

PSALMS 30:5

Weeping may go on all night, but in the
morning there is joy.

Rejoice! As a Christian your days of mourning
are gone forever!

PSALMS 30:11

Then he turned my sorrow into joy!
He took away my clothes of mourning and
clothed me with joy.

If you honor the Lord He will provide
for your every need!

PSALMS 34:10

Even strong young lions sometimes
go hungry, but those of us who reverence the
Lord will never lack any good thing.

Do not lose hope, God is faithful to rescue
His children from their distress!

PSALMS 35:9

But I will rejoice in the Lord.
He shall rescue me!

Everyone can receive the joy of the Lord!

PSALMS 40:16

But may the joy of the Lord be given
to everyone who loves him and his salvation.
May they constantly
exclaim, "How great God is!"

God will quench your spiritual thirst and bathe
you in joy with His divine love!

PSALMS 46:4

There is a river of joy flowing
through the City of our God—the sacred home
of the God above all gods.

Our Lord is gracious and quick to forgive those
who sin against Him!

PSALMS 51:8

And after you have punished me, give me
back my joy again.

Restoration belongs to you no matter how
damaged the condition of your soul!

PSALMS 53:6

Only when the Lord himself restores them can
they ever be really happy again.

God will carry all of your burdens for you!

PSALMS 55:22

Give your burdens to the Lord.
He will carry them.
He will not permit the godly to slip or fall.

No matter how bleak your circumstances
seem in the dark of night,
the Lord will place a song of encouragement in
your heart to greet the new day!

PSALMS 57:8

Rouse yourself, my soul!
Arise, O harp and lyre! Let us greet the
dawn with song!

God is busy looking out for your well-being and
best interests each minute of every day!

PSALMS 69:32

The humble shall see their God at
work for them. No wonder they will be so glad!
All who seek for God shall live in joy.

Your emptiness will be filled with
the blessings of the Lord!

PSALMS 81:10

For it was I, Jehovah your God,
who brought you out of the land of Egypt.
Only test me! Open your mouth wide
and see if I won't fill it. You will receive every
blessing you can use!

You will never stumble around
in darkness and uncertainty for the Lord
will shine His light on
every good thing around you!

PSALMS 84:11

For Jehovah God is our Light
and our Protector. He gives us grace and glory.
No good thing will he withhold
from those who walk along his paths.

God will turn your tears and sadness into
songs of joyous praise!

PSALMS 126:5

Those who sow tears shall reap joy.
Yes, they go out weeping
carrying seed for sowing, and return singing,
carrying their sheaves.

God has a plan for your life!

PSALMS 138:8

The Lord will work out his plans
for my life—for your lovingkindness,
Lord, continues forever.
Don't abandon me—for you made me.

You can face every spiritual conflict with the skill of an experienced warrior!

PSALMS 144:1

Bless the Lord who is my immovable Rock. He gives me strength and skill in battle.

God promises to
always love and protect you!

PSALMS 144:2

He is always kind and loving to me;
he is my fortress, my tower of strength and
safety, my deliverer. He stands before me
as a shield. He subdues my people under me.

God will never disappoint you by
breaking His promises!

PSALMS 146:6b, 7

He is the God who keeps every promise,
and gives justice to the poor and oppressed, and
food to the hungry.

Your acts of kindness and goodness will be
eternally rewarded!

PROVERBS 10:28

The hope of good men is eternal happiness.

You will *experience* untold blessings in your
life when you honor the Lord!

PROVERBS 19:23

Reverence for God gives life, happiness, and
protection from harm.

No man or woman can ever
truly harm you!

PROVERBS 16:7

When a man is trying to please God,
God makes even his worst enemies to be at
peace with him.

No one will be able to
manipulate you with false charm
and flattery!

PROVERBS 29:5-6

Flattery is a trap;
evil men are caught in it, but good men stay
away and sing for joy.

You don't have to worry about
being a failure—God will reward your integrity
with many blessings!

ECCLESIASTES 2:26

For God give those who please him wisdom,
knowledge, and joy; but if a
sinner becomes wealthy, God takes the wealth
away from him and
gives it to those who please him.

Each day of your life is a gift from God!

ECCLESIASTES 11:8

If a person lives to be very old,
let him rejoice in every day of life, but let him
also remember that eternity is
far longer, and that everything down here is
futile in comparison.

God is especially generous with those
who are in great need!

ISAIAH 29:19

The meek will be filled with fresh joy from
the Lord, and the poor
shall exalt in the Holy One of Israel.

Your praises to the Lord will fill your
own heart with joy!

ISAIAH 30:29

But the people of God will sing a song
of solemn joy, like songs in the night when holy
feasts are held; his people will have
gladness of heart, as when a flutist leads a
pilgrim band to Jerusalem to the
Mountain of the Lord, the Rock of Israel.

Even when you don't feel the presence
of the Lord, He is still there—filling your life
with His fragrant blessings!

ISAIAH 35:1

Even the wilderness and desert will
rejoice in those days; the desert will blossom
with flowers.

You will glory in the joy of the Lord!

ISAIAH 41:16

And the joy of the Lord shall fill you full;
you shall glory in the God of Israel.

The Lord will continue to bless you through
your children!

ISAIAH 44:3

For I will give you abundant water for your
thirst and for your parched fields.
And I will pour out my Spirit and my blessings
on your children.

All of creation rejoices
at your salvation!

ISAIAH 55:12

You will live in joy and peace.
The mountains and hills, the trees of the field—
all the world around you—will rejoice.

You will never have to experience
shame or despair!

ISAIAH 61:7

Instead of shame and dishonor,
you shall have a double portion of prosperity
and everlasting joy.

Even in the midst of sorrow you will experience the joy of the Lord!

JEREMIAH 31:25

For I have given rest to the weary and joy to all the sorrowing.

God is refining and perfecting
you each day!

EZEKIEL 11:19

I will give you one heart and a new spirit;
I will take from you
your hearts of stone and give you tender
hearts of love for God.

Everything that happens in the world is under
the control of the Lord your God!

DANIEL 2:21

World events are under his control.
He removes kings and sets others on their
thrones. He gives wise men
their wisdom, and scholars their intelligence.

Your faith will give you the ability
to do great things!

DANIEL 11:32

He will flatter those who hate the things of God,
and win them over to his side.
But the people who know their God shall be
strong and do great things.

God has made your heart His home!

ZECHARIAH 2:10

"Sing, Jerusalem, and rejoice! For I have come
to live among you," says the Lord.

Jesus is willing
to carry your burdens so you can rest
in His presence!

MATTHEW 11:28

Come to me and I will
give you rest—all of you who work so hard
beneath a heavy yoke.

The Lord has given you a vital role
in His Kingdom!

MATTHEW 25:21

His master praised him for good work.
"You have been faithful in handling the small
amount," he told him, "so now I will give
you many more responsibilities.
Begin the joyous tasks I have assigned you."

God sent His Son so that you would never
have to be afraid of anything!

LUKE 2:10

But the angel reassured them.
"Don't be afraid!" he said. "I bring you
the most joyful news
ever announced, and it is for everyone!"

A great reward is waiting for you in heaven!

LUKE 6:22-23

What happiness it is when others hate you and exclude you and insult you and smear your name because you are mine! When that happens, rejoice! Yes, leap for joy! For you will have a great reward awaiting you in heaven. And you will be in good company—the ancient prophets were treated that way too!

You cannot lose what the Lord has given you!

JOHN 16:22

You have sorrow now, but I will
see you again and then you will rejoice;
and no one can rob you of that joy.

You can ask your Heavenly Father
for anything!

JOHN 16:24

You haven't tried this before,
(but begin now). Ask, using my name,
and you will receive,
and your cup of joy will overflow.

Peace of mind belongs to you because Jesus
has defeated all of your sadness!

JOHN 16:33

I have told you all this so that you will
have peace of heart and mind.
Here on earth you will have many trials and
sorrows; but cheer up,
for I have overcome the world.

You are a person of
highest privilege in the glorious and
eternal Kingdom of God!

ROMANS 5:2

For because of our faith, he has brought us
into this place of highest privilege
where we now stand, and we confidently and
joyfully look forward to
actually becoming all that God has had
in mind for us to be.

God loves you so much He wants to be your
friend forever!

ROMANS 5:11

Now we rejoice in our wonderful relationship
with God—all because of what our
Lord Jesus Christ has done in dying for our sins—
making us friends of God.

Jesus has conquered death for your sake!

ROMANS 5:17

The sin of this one man, Adam,
caused death to be king over all, but all who
will take God's gift of forgiveness
and acquittal are kings of life because of this
one man, Jesus Christ.

The Lord has borne your sins
on the cross so that you can live in
His presence forever!

ROMANS 5:18

Yes, Adam's sin brought punishment
to all, but Christ's righteousness makes men
right with God, so that they can live.

You do not have to pay even one penny for
eternal life!

ROMANS 6:23

For the wages of sin is death,
but the free gift of God is eternal life through
Jesus Christ our Lord.

God's promises to you will never change!

ROMANS 11:29

For God's gifts and his call
can never be withdrawn; he will never go
back on his promises.

God has given you special abilities and gifts!

ROMANS 12:6

God has given each of us the ability to do
certain things well.

God has a unique and glorious purpose
for your life!

ROMANS 12:12

Be glad for all God is planning for you.

The Lord will nourish and refresh your spirit
with His glorious presence!

ROMANS 14:17

For, after all, the important thing
for us as Christians is not what we eat or drink
but stirring up goodness
and peace and joy from the Holy Spirit.

Your thoughts, words, and actions are directed
by the truths of God's Word!

1 CORINTHIANS 1:5

He has enriched your whole life.
He has helped you speak out for him and has
given you a full understanding of the truth.

You can share with other people the richness of God's blessings!

2 CORINTHIANS 6:10

Our hearts ache, but at the same time we have the joy of the Lord. We are poor, but we give rich spiritual gifts to others. We own nothing, and yet we enjoy everything.

God will continue to bless you in the midst of sorrow and uncertainty!

2 CORINTHIANS 7:4

I have the highest confidence in you, and my pride in you is great. You have greatly encouraged me; you have made me so happy in spite of all my suffering.

God will provide you with such
an abundance of joy that even when times
are tough you will be able
to share His blessings with others!

2 CORINTHIANS 8:2

Though they have been going through much
trouble and hard times, they have
mixed their wonderful joy with their deep
poverty, and the result
has been an overflow of giving to others.

God is using your life to bless other people!

2 CORINTHIANS 9:8

God is able to make it up to you by giving you everything you need and more, so that there will not only be enough for your own needs, but plenty left over to give joyfully to others.

Satan has no power over your life!

2 CORINTHIANS 10:4

I use God's mighty weapons,
not those made by men, to knock down the
devil's strongholds.

God has turned your weakness into strength!

> 2 CORINTHIANS 12:10

Since I know it is all for Christ's good,
I am quite happy about
"the thorn," and about insults and hardships,
persecutions and difficulties;
for when I am weak, then I am strong—the less
I have, the more I depend on him.

Your life is directed by the One who
desires only the best for you!

GALATIANS 5:22a

But when the Holy Spirit controls our
lives he will produce this kind of fruit in us:
love, joy, peace.

God is working for you in ways that
you can't even imagine!

EPHESIANS 3:20

Now glory be to God who by his mighty
power at work within us is able to do far more
than we would ever dare to ask or even
dream of—infinitely beyond our highest prayers,
desires, thoughts, or hopes.

God is helping you obey Him in
all areas of your life!

PHILIPPIANS 2:13

For God is at work within you,
helping you want to obey him, and then
helping you do what he wants.

While the rest of the world is in turmoil,
your heart is quiet and
your thoughts are filled with peace!

PHILIPPIANS 4:7

If you do this you will experience God's peace,
which is far more wonderful than
the human mind can understand. His peace
will keep your thoughts and your hearts
quiet and at rest as you trust in Christ Jesus.

Your God will never die!

1 TIMOTHY 1:17

Glory and honor to God forever and ever.
He is the King of the ages,
the unseen one who never dies; he alone is God,
and full of wisdom. Amen.

No matter what challenges you face,
God will give you the
strength to endure and succeed!

COLOSSIANS 1:11

We are praying, too, that you will be filled
with his mighty, glorious strength so that you
can keep going no matter what
happens—always full of the joy of the Lord.

God lives inside of you!

HEBREWS 3:6

But Christ, God's faithful Son, is in complete
charge of God's house. And we
Christians are God's house—he lives in us!—
if we keep up our courage firm to
the end, and our joy and our trust in the Lord.

Jesus will share everything that
He possesses with you!

HEBREWS 3:14

For if we are faithful to the end,
trusting God just as we did when we first
became Christians, we will
share in all that belongs to Christ.

Your problems and needs are
meaningless in comparison to the riches that
await you in heaven!

HEBREWS 10:34

You suffered with those thrown into jail,
and you were actually joyful
when all you owned was taken from you,
knowing that better things were
awaiting you in heaven, things that would
be yours forever.

You are able to face overwhelming
adversity with great joy!

JAMES 1:2

Dear brothers, is your life full of
difficulties and temptations? Then be happy.

The Lord never becomes impatient with
you or your needs!

JAMES 5:13

Is anyone among you suffering?
He should keep on praying about it. And those
who have reason to be thankful should
continually be singing praises to the Lord.

You are a vital member of God's family!

1 PETER 1:3

All honor to God, the God and Father of
our Lord Jesus Christ; for it is his
boundless mercy that has given us the privilege
of being born again, so that we are now
members of God's own family. Now we live in
the hope of eternal life because Christ rose
again from the dead.

The good life is yours because Jesus has
shared His glory with you!

2 PETER 1:3

For as you know him better, he will give you,
through his great power, everything
you need for living a truly good life: he even
shares his own glory and his
own goodness with us!

You are a close,
personal friend of Jesus Christ!

2 PETER 3:18

But grow in spiritual strength and become
better acquainted with our Lord
and Savior Jesus Christ. To him be all glory
and splendid honor,
both now and forevermore. Good-bye.

Jesus has washed you perfectly clean
from the stain of sin!

1 JOHN 1:9

But if we confess our sins to him, he can be
depended on to forgive us and to
cleanse us from every wrong. (And it is
perfectly proper for God to do
this for us because Christ died to wash
away our sins.)

Each day with the Lord brings you closer
and closer to perfection!

JUDE 1:25

And he is able to keep you from slipping and
falling away, and to bring you, sinless
and perfect, into his glorious presence with
mighty shouts of everlasting joy.

You are an important part
of God's Kingdom!

REVELATION 1:6

He has gathered us into
his kingdom and made us priests of God his
Father. Give to him
everlasting glory! He rules forever! Amen!

One day you will wear
a crown that is more valuable than gold and
will never tarnish or fade!

REVELATION 2:10

Remain faithful even when
facing death and I will give you the crown of
life—an unending, glorious future.

One day the whole world will join you to worship the Living God!

REVELATION 15:3-4

And they were singing the song of Moses, the servant of God, and the song of the Lamb: "Great and marvelous are your doings, Lord God Almighty. Just and true are your ways, O King of Ages. Who shall not fear, O Lord, and glorify your Name? For you alone are holy. All nations will come and worship before you, for your righteous deeds have been disclosed."